Ho ... AT
To ... AP

UNCO ... ON

Color Illustrations by Hugh Whyte

ANDIRON PRESS

East Hanover, New Jersey

DISCARD

I

HOW TO GET A CAT TO SIT IN YOUR LAP.
Copyright ©1995 by D. Michael Denny.
B&W illustrations copyright ©1995 by Carol Morgan.
Color illustrations copyright ©1995 by Hugh Whyte.

ANDIRON PRESS

Publisher's Cataloging in Publication
(Prepared by Quality Books Inc.)
Denny, D. Michael
How to get a cat to sit in your lap –: confessions of an
unconventional cat person / by D.Michael Denny ;
illustrated by Carol Morgan – 1st ed.
p. cm.
ISBN 0-9645799-0-1
1. Cats–Humor.   I. Morgan, Carol, ill.   II. Title.
SF445.5.D46 1995   636.8
QBI95-20076

Library of Congress Catalog Card Number: 95-94275

ATTENTION SCHOOLS AND CORPORATIONS:
Quantity discounts are available on bulk purchases of this book.
For information, contact:
Marketing Department,
Andiron Press, P.O. Box 303, East Hanover, NJ 07936

Graphic design and color art by Lehner & Whyte, Inc., Montclair, NJ 07042
Printed by Commercial Reprographics, Inc., Plainfield, NJ 07060

Acknowledgement

Sometimes the secret to survival is the support (moral and otherwise) of good friends. So, to Mom; Al & Em; Tom & George; Mac & Judy; Rich; Phil & Carol; Ed & Gloria; Bill & Eileen; Lehner & Whyte; Jim; Commercial Reprographics; Sage Editorial; Harry; Kent & Pru; Dick & Adrienne; Don & Mary; Pastor Dale; Father Harvey; and Jim; Bill; Walt, and the rest of the guys in the band – on behalf of a grateful Denny family – thank you!

Dedication

To Zooby, Scruffy, Gypsy, Poor Henry, and the other
cats and kittens that slipped through the
net, eluding our care and comfort.

Table of Contents

GlenDenny
Built in 1783

Born in La Salle, Illinois, in 1938, Michael graduated in the upper third of his class (alphabetically) from the University of Illinois, English Lit. major, in 1962. That same year, he went on to the Navy's Officer Candidate School, where he received a commission as Ensign (despite his commanding officer's outraged protestations).

D. Michael Denny, *sans* cat (as usual)
Photo by William Ringlieb

In 1965, Michael began an advertising writing career in the San Francisco office of Young & Rubicam. He moved to New York City in 1968, to New Jersey in 1973, and in 1984 became a full-time free lance writer, billing himself as "the second-best writer in New Jersey."

Today, Michael lives in East Hanover, New Jersey, with his wife, Nancy, three daughters, six cats, and one nervous iguana – who doesn't answer to the name J.R. Michael's avocational interests include cooking (with an Italian accent) and traditional jazz. (He's played clarinet for over 40 years, and is the leader of the Centennial Jazz Band (*"If it ain't hot, it's not!"*)

In 1990, while serving on the Board of Directors of the New Jersey Jazz Society, he conceived and coordinated the Centennial of Jazz, which was celebrated worldwide on June 10, 1990. In 1991, he established International Jazz Day, which is celebrated worldwide each year on the Saturday of the Memorial Day weekend in May. Michael offers no excuse for any of this.

Introduction

"Stately, kindly, lordly friend
Condescend Here
to sit by me."

To a Cat
by
Algernon Charles Swinburne

For the record, I'll be the first to admit that I am not one of those chosen few to whom cats come running for company or affection. There is no natural or supra natural empathy between cats and myself. None of the six who presently share my life competes to sit in (or on) my lap. Like most of you, I am resigned to be merely an accepted presence in their existence. But I am not offended by this. Honest.

Those who know tell me that this book is probably *not* the first cat book you've ever read. Therefore, since I am addressing a reasonably knowledgeable audience, I'm not too worried about being a possible source of (unintentional) misinformation.

How to Get a Cat to Sit in Your Lap is not a compendium of dry data. It does not force-feed you psychologically-correct character profiles of the Japanese Bobtail versus Maine Coon cats. Nor does it regale you with a verbose explanation of the form and function of the feline vomeronasal (sniffing) organ. And it most certainly does not dwell on the mating habits of the cat – since every cat I've owned has been either spayed or neutered. (Besides, from what I've seen on the various TV soaps my daughters watch, we human types have no right to be critical.) Instead, in this book I've chosen to share with you the highly personal (and shamelessly subjective) observations and conclusions accumulated after almost thirty years of close interaction with cats.

And, to those skeptics among you who are idly perusing this book while pondering its purchase, you have my assurance that within these pages I *will*, in fact, provide you with the answer to that age-old question: "How do you get a cat to sit in your lap?" – eschewing rude force or drugs, of course.

What? Oh, ye of little faith . . .

D. Michael Denny

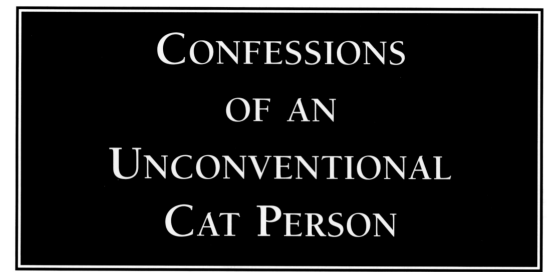

Chapter 1

CONFESSIONS OF AN UNCONVENTIONAL CAT PERSON

The first thing you should know is, I didn't get into this cat bag voluntarily. My introduction to living a cat-driven life was compelled by my youthful, right-brain love/lust for a beguiling farmer's daughter and aspiring artist who, as it turned out, had grown up with *Felis catus*. My wife Nancy was, and always has been an unabashed *felinophile* (cat lover). Her childhood on her parents' Maryland farm was an isolated one. There were no playmates next door, or even down the road. Therefore, she created her own fantasy land, populated with a seemingly endless variety of furry-purry friends with names like Ginger, Tommy, and Smoky.

When she was six or seven, Nancy tells me she and her "friends" would get all dressed up and have tea parties. Or, she would put them all in her wagon, and they'd go on dangerous safari through the woods behind the barn. As she got older, their role in her life changed from playmates to companions, and eventually to confidants. So you see, my wife Nancy is a cat person, born and bred.

I, on the other hand, was the original boy-with-a-dog. I must have had four or five by the time I was sixteen. I still have strong memories of one of the first . . .

My very bestest friend . . .

In that dream-distant spring in 1944 in La Salle, Illinois, I was just five years old, getting ready to start kindergarten (whatever *that* was).

I remember, I was standing on the sidewalk near the kitchen door of my parents' tavern when I spotted a large dog loping down the block toward me. Even at that age, I could tell it was a "he," and I could also tell he hadn't eaten recently. (I know now he was a short-haired pointer of some sort – white with brown spots.)

"What's the matter, boy? You lost, fella? Want something to eat?" Eat! Now that was a word the dog understood. He stopped, looked into my eyes and wagged his tail.

"Hey Mom," I yelled as I ran into the kitchen. There, my mother, formerly Della Mancini, of the Mark, Illinois, Mancinis, was rolling out pasta dough for the incredible homemade, meat-filled tortellini we served at Denny's Tavern. "Mom, can I have a piece of salami?" This was not an unusual request. Even in 1944 I recognized that Genoa salami was one of man's stellar culinary achievements. To this day it remains an integral part of my essential sensory appreciation. (And never mind what it does to my blood pressure.)

Salami in hand, I ran back outside to find the dog waiting patiently for me. I gave him my salami, and he gave me his love. Did he ever! From that day on he was my constant companion. I named him "Spotty." (Hey, what do you want? I was five years old, for Pete's sake!)

Now the thing about Spotty was, he was convinced I was the ideal boy! (Actually, it was an opinion we *both* shared.) However, as often happens in life, reality would occasionally intrude – usually in the form of an open-handed glancing blow off the side of my head; delivered by my mother when *her* perception of my behavior registered as something less than ideal.

(For the edification of my younger readers, in 1944, whacking an unruly little kid off the side of the head was *not* considered child abuse. On the contrary, it was generally regarded as a re-affirmation of familial affection. And, while I may have occasionally received more than one whack a day, I hardly ever recall getting more than one in succession. [Of course, the unfortunate events which took place the day the garage burned down were an exception to the rule, but that's another story.])

Anyway, when Spotty entered the picture, things changed dramatically for me. From that day on, anyone – parent, friend, or stranger – who held malice-aforethought for young Michael could only get at me by braving the bared fangs and no-nonsense growl of good old you-know-who. Suddenly, I was invulnerable! Immune from the reflexive retaliations of my mother – or any one or anything else for that matter.

In retrospect, the simple fact is, for the first (and last) time of my life, I was loved *unequivocally* and *without qualification*. Ah, Spotty, dear Spotty. You should have lived forever.

One other quick young-Denny/dog story. (I *know* this is supposed to be a book about cats. I just feel it's important for you to understand that even though I didn't grow up with cats, as a child, I was exposed to certain seminal learning experiences which transcended a world of slot machines and short beers!)

Oh, boy!

By the summer of 1954, Denny's Tavern had been relocated about 70 miles northeast of La Salle in Wasco, Illinois. The family now included my seven-year-old sister, Susan, while the resident canine in the household was a 3½-foot tall, 136-pound, eight-year-old male pedigreed Great Dane (whose credentials put both sides of my family's linage to shame).

This majestic paragon of the breed had just come into our lives. His appearance was the product of (1) a heart-rending story by a well-to-do customer of my parents' tavern who was being forced to move out-of-state *sans* dog, and (2) the sympathetic offering of a case of his favorite Scotch (the customer's, not the dog's) by one Peter J. Denny (my father). The booze was accompanied by a pledge to provide above-said dog with the quality of life to which the aristocratic canine had become accustomed.

(No one could ever say my father didn't mean well. I can remember at least two other dogs, a cross-eyed horse, and a homicidal pony who found themselves unexpectedly clutched to our family bosom in that halcyon era – all a direct result of my father's case-of-Scotch gambit, or some variation thereof.)

At first, Boy fit into our family scenario as well as any clumsy behemoth squeezed into a modest five-room home might be expected. However, before very long, certain idiosyncrasies in Boy's behavioral patterns began to emerge, quickly altering our lives.

Idiosyncrasy number one revealed itself on a sultry afternoon during one of our not infrequent Illinois summer storms. At the first startling clap of thunder, Boy, who was in the yard with me, bolted toward the front door of the house. True, the door was closed, but a screen door designed to keep out flies and mosquitoes is no match for a panic-stricken 136-pound Great Dane in full flight.

After some reflection,* I advised my father of the incident, and helped him search the house for Boy. Finding a large dog in a small house is a more difficult task than you might think when the animal in question is being driven by a desperate instinct to survive.

Eventually, though, we found him – cowering in our little bathroom, wedged behind the toilet. Threats, pleadings, temptations of fresh chicken giblets, nothing would pry him from his refuge. It was hours after the storm had passed before Boy emerged, looking a little sheepish, but by no means apologetic.

A few weeks later, my father was to experience Boy's fear of thunderstorms up-close and personal, as they say. On this memorable occasion, Dad was seated in the bathroom, placidly perusing a copy of Field and Stream when the first loud thunderclap struck. Fortunately, this time the outside screen door was open. *Unfortunately* (and unbeknownst to my father), the bathroom door was ajar. Before he could comprehend (much less react to) the clattering sound of the crazed beast's huge paws racing down the linoleum hallway, Golden Boy came hurtling through the bathroom door; knocking my father off his contemplative throne, and wedging *both* of them behind the toilet. (It's a good thing Dad was a dog lover.)

*Ever since the previously mentioned destruction by fire of the Denny family garage in 1947 (and the predictably painful consequences that followed), I've been loath to be the bearer of bad news to authority figures.

Chapter 2

SEDUCED BY THE QUEEN OF THE CAT CLAN

As you've seen, my formative years were totally free of any feline experiences. Unlike Nancy, I was raised with *Canis familiaris*, a pet who *came* when you called; who *defended* when you were threatened; who *grieved* when you were away; who *rejoiced* upon your return, and who *obeyed* when you commanded. I was, in a phrase, a dog person. To me, a cat was an unknown quantity. Then, on the first Thursday of April, 1963, in Philadelphia, I met and fell into the arms of Nancy: Queen of the Cat Clan, and my fate was sealed.

Today, the Denny family lives on the almost-one-acre family "estate" I call GlenDenny. There's Nancy and me, our three daughters, six cats, and one nervous iguana named J.R. I believe introductions are in order, since you never know when one or more of them may pop into view.

Your humble author is: D. Michael Denny. (No, I won't tell you what the "D." stands for.)

D. Michael Denny: AKA Dad, Michael, Mr. Denny, and "You sweet thing you . . ." Born: 4/24/38, La Salle, Illinois. Profession: free lance advertising writer. (If this isn't enough of a profile for you, see the *Author, Author* page.)

Nancy Ann (Rogge) Denny: AKA Mom, "Nance," Mrs. Denny, and "Sweetheart" (used all too infrequently, according to her). *"Age cannot wither, nor custom stale. . ."* etc., etc. Born in Baltimore, Maryland, Nancy is a compelling, blond-haired blue-eyed first-generation American of Germanic parentage. As previously noted, she was raised on a farm in northern Maryland and is a graduate of Moore College of Art in Philadelphia. We met on a blind date arranged by one of her classmates, whom she hasn't spoken to since.

Nancy regards our cats as family, not pets, and believes they need to be kissed every day. She works as a wallpaper and window treatment specialist at The Home Depot here in town. Her hobbies are garage sales (going and having) and making lists. All in all, she'd rather be an international traveler.

The Kids:

Clarissa Ann Denny: AKA "Dammit Clarissa!" and "ClarissAAAA!" Petite with blond hair and, like all of our daughters, greenish-blue eyes, Clarissa marked her twenty-second birthday last August. Some children are non-achievers; others are over-achievers; and still others are under-achievers. Clarissa adds a whole new subset to the genre: the anti-achiever.

A year after graduating (in the broadest sense of the term) from high school, she left home to join the Circus as a trick horse rider – having absolutely no experience with either show biz or riding. The first thing she learned about working around horses was that she was allergic to them! (No, this is not my idea of cheap humor. This is the kind of thing that passes for reality around here.)

She's back home now, awash in Heavy Metal music; collecting a startling variety of long-haired young males and living with her iguana, J.R., in our spare room. At least in her present job, an assembler of electronic components, she hasn't demonstrated any symptoms of being allergic to soldering irons.

Amanda Maria Denny: AKA "Manda." Also petite, but with red hair, Amanda turned eighteen last August; graduated with honors* from high school, Class of '94, and is now attending junior college. Most outstanding personality trait: world class stubbornness, complemented by a smart mouth. She's an apocalyptic example of the apple which doesn't fall very far from the tree.

As a result of working part-time as a word processor, she drives a fully-loaded, five-year-old Dodge Daytona. (Meanwhile, I'm lucky to be driving an almost completely unloaded thirteen-year-old Toyota Tercel!) Her car boasts a window sticker which urges: *"Save the planet. Kill yourself!"*

Unless she shapes up, Amanda is in clear danger of following in the footsteps of her father – one whom society deems to be somewhat amusing, but a bit much.

Emily Louise Adel Denny: AKA "Emmy." Another redhead, Emily is a bright (High Honors** in her freshman year) and precocious sixteen-year-old, as tall as her mother (5′6″), and making good bucks at her after-school job. ("She looks like some cousins I grew up with," my father had observed. "The only real Denny in the bunch!" [To anyone who knows the genealogy, a *very* mixed blessing.])

Emily has a great love for our cats, as well as fireflies, birds, raccoons, ground hogs, and bats. All are worthy of her interest and concern. Unfortunately, this lovely phase of her life is too good to last. At some point, due to peer pressure, or some socio/sexual revelation, my rare butterfly will probably metamorphose into a more typical teenager – but, I predict, a very lovely one.

*Heredity **can** work!

**Heredity works!!

The Cats:

1. Sadat: AKA "Sadat Sweetpants" - Like all of our cats, a domestic shorthair. He's a brown tabby, thirteen years old with yellow eyes and a pink nose; possessing a paranoid personality, with a persecution complex which, in some ways, is entirely justified. At one time he was afflicted with advanced wanderlust, but since he came home with near fatal arrow wounds last year, he has decided there's no place like home.*

Motto: *"Why do they keep staring at me? What do they want from me?"*

Hobby: Worrying.

Origin: Came to us as a kitten; a "gift" from an overly generous neighbor. At the same time we adopted Cleopatra, now one of the Clearly Departed. (See next page)

2. Tristan: AKA "Twiddles" or "Tristie" - Another brown male tabby, but with white markings. Ten years old, with green eyes and a pink nose, Tristan is the King of GlenDenny. He's a cat's cat, with a melancholy expression, a ruthless reputation among local chipmunks, and a $800 stainless steel plate in his hip.

Motto: *"I'm number one."*

Hobby: Lording it over the others – especially Bart.

Origin: Paws Animal Shelter, Montclair, New Jersey. Found abandoned as a kitten on a busy NJ Interstate.

3. Pizza: AKA "Peetie" - A distinctly overweight orange female tabby with a white-undercarriage. Nine years old, with orange eyes, and a pink and brown nose, biologically, she's a very unusual cat. The vast majority of orange tabbies are *males*. (This has been pointed out to Pizza on several occasions, but she could care less.)

Motto: *"Call me anything you like, just don't call me late for dinner."*

Hobby: Eating.

Origin: Discovered, hungry and in heat, hanging around the garbage container of a pizza franchise in Nutley, New Jersey.

No, it wasn't Indians. Here in East Hanover, the last member of the Lenni Lenape tribe was seen hanging around Cook's Inn in 1824. This murderous assault was the handywork of a local juvenile delinquent who, I expect, will soon be starring on <u>America's Most Wanted</u> TV show.

4. Scamper: AKA "Scampi" or "Pampers" - A silver male tabby, seven years old; enormous green eyes, a brown nose, and a neurotic nature. He's been known to bite people on the ankle to get their attention – or just because he feels like it. (It's all Clarissa's fault. She used to roughhouse with him when he was a kitten. Nancy and I thought it was cute, at the time.) Scamper's the only one of our cats even vaguely interested in our swimming pool. He likes hanging over the edge and drinking from it. (You'll be happy to know that cats can swim – if they *have* to.)
Motto: *"Don't tread on me!"*
Hobby: Staring.
Origin: East Hanover Animal Shelter.

5. Pumpkin: AKA "Punky" - An orange male tabby, five years old; orange eyes and a tawny-colored nose. Was doing fine until Bart came along. Now lives in hiding somewhere in the house.
Motto: *"I think five cats were perfect for this family!"*
Hobby: Looking over his right (and left) shoulder.
Origin: Rescued by Clarissa from a boy friend's "My landlord won't let me keep my cat!" situation.

6. Barthalemew: AKA "Bart." A large black male, yellow eyes, with a gentle disposition for everyone (except Punky). At four years old, Bart is the likely successor to Tristan as the Leader of the Pack. (At least, Tristan seems to think so.)
Motto: *"My harvest too will come."*
Hobby: Making Punky's life interesting.
Origin: A gratuitous gift from one of Clarissa's boy friends (a different one) who was being thrown out of his apartment for unspecified acts against the state.

(NOTE: Other members of our Clearly Departed Cat Club: Pekoe, Missy, Rosebud, Dandy, Shiney, Dotty, Daisy, and Sheba.
Rest in Peace, kiddos.)

Chapter 3

PROTO-CAT, ITS PROGENY, AND THEIR PLACE IN HISTORY

Just for the record, the first earthly ancestor of today's cat was the Miacis. This weasel-like proto-mammal first appeared on earth some forty million years ago in the Eocene epoch. He was one of the first carnivores on earth, and proud of it!

Unfortunately, its competition in the meat-eating department in those days was several hundred species of dinosaur – some, the size of a cross-town bus. As a result, every day the <u>Jurassic Park</u> scenario was the rule rather than the exception for poor little Miacis.

Motivated by this hostile environment, one branch of the Miacis family decided to gradually evolve into a distinctly more cat-like entity: the Civet – who, unwilling to leave well enough alone – insisted on eventually becoming the cat as we now know it. (I use the word "know" in the figurative, as opposed to the literal, sense of course.)

Meanwhile, another branch of the Miacis family had its little heart set on becoming dogs – and, after an eon or two, they did. (The hardest part was learning to "fetch.")

The licking phenomenon originated with the first feline carnivores millions of years ago. They discovered that if they kept themselves well-washed, their prey couldn't smell them as easily. Which might raise the question, "How often should today's cat have a bath?" A little less often than Marie Antoinette, I'd say.

The evolution of a vendetta . . .

By extending the above evolutionary pattern to its logical conclusion, I believe I've isolated the original source of the eternal antipathy which has existed between cats and birds since time immemorial. To wit: I believe today's birds evolved from yesterday's dinosaurs, and today's cat is haunted by residual memories – buried deep in its primeval cortex. Memories of *persecution* in pre-cretaceous ages.

My proof? Consider: In recent years, science has determined that dinosaurs were warm-blooded reptiles. Also, it's generally accepted that the first flying critters evolved from reptiles. Almost certainly, for millions of years, those first avian carnivores considered early mammals a legitimate part of their menu. Perhaps even a delicacy!

Cut to the present. A cat is walking through the garden. Suddenly, it freezes, and sinks into an attack crouch. Why? Because it has seen a bird, unsuspecting and vulnerable. From deep within the cat's primitive psyche comes the ancient memory: the daily massacre of its proto-cat forebears by flying reptiles. Airborn monstrosities like *Nyctosaurus, Pteranodon, Rhamporhynchus*, and utimately, *Archaeoptereyx*, the first flying reptile to decide to opt for feathers instead of scales. "Vengeance is mine," saith the cat, seeking retribution. (A concept not altogether unknown in certain parts of Staten Island.) Anyway, back to the chronology . . .

Enter cat, stage left, chasing rat . . .

It is believed that cats have been tolerating the presence of man for about five thousand years. It probably all started in ancient Egypt, where cats were worshiped and venerated. To an Egyptian, a cat sleeping with its body curled up, its head touching its tail, was the perfect symbol for eternity. Also, to Egyptians, cats were considered sacred to Isis, who represented the moon. Their chief goddess, Bast [or Bastet, or Pasht, or Bubastis, or – oh, never mind), who represented life-giving solar heat, was portrayed with a cat's head. And, I'll bet you didn't know the first historical reference to a cat was found on an ancient tablet, written in Sanskrit. It was a recipe! (Just kidding. Just kidding!)

Herodotus, in his "History," reports that cats were so highly regarded in Egypt, people would risk their lives by running into a burning house to save them. And, according to no less an authority than Diodorus, the law of Egypt declared that killing a cat, even by accident, was punishable by death! So was smuggling a cat out of the country! (And you wonder why *Felis catus* has such a high opinion of himself.) Incidentally, the Egyptian word for cat was *Mau*. Perhaps the most outstanding example of onomatopoeic usage (the creation of words in imitation of natural sounds) in history.

But here's the most *revealing* data bit on the prestige of cats in ancient Egypt is this. When a favorite cat died in ancient Egypt, it was mummified in the same way as any other Egyptian, and was even buried in its own little tomb! (With little mummified mice to keep it company, no doubt!)

NOTE: Since I first wrote this *bon mot*, I've come to learn that the Egyptians did, in fact, bury mummified mice along with their cats! It just goes to show how often what passes for contemporary wit, can pale before the ironies of history.

But the question remains – just why *did* the Egyptians venerate cats to such an extraordinary degree? Simple. Their gods didn't work, and cats did! For example, around 3,000 B.C., the business of the day in Egypt was raising grain (the fertile Valley of the Nile and all that). As you might expect, Egypt was filled with granaries. Unfortunately, the granaries were filled with mice and/or rats. For the average Egyptian, the result was wholesale malnutrition. Enter a cat, chasing a rat. The grain was saved, and the ancient Egyptians were so grateful they celebrated their salvation by making war upon their neighbors.

More days in the sun . . .

Moving right along, the ancient Romans also owned cats, as did the Phoenicians and the Etruscans before them. Like the Egyptians, the Romans passed a law protecting cats. However, they were much more pragmatic about the role of the cat in Roman society. They used the cat as a symbol of liberty and let it go at that.

These early civilizations, by taking their cats with them as they carved out their empires, allowed the once geographically restricted cat to really begin getting around.

Controversy still abounds whether it was Hywel Dda, the Prince of South Wales, or the King of Wales, Howell the Good, who set the value of a cat throughout its life. (You've probably run across this from your other readings.) "From birth to when it opens its eyes: 1 penny. After that, until it kills its first mouse: 2 pennies. After it proves itself as a successful mouse hunter: 4 pennies." Now if that doesn't sound like a lot of money to you, remember, a penny went a lot farther in 936 A.D. And mice were cheaper then too.

Regarding who actually created this ancient value system – from my own experiences after almost thirty years in the advertising business, I'd bet the Prince came up with the idea, and the King took credit for it.

Centuries later, in medieval Japan, only members of the Imperial Court were allowed to own cats. They kept them on leashes, probably so the cats wouldn't have a chance to do what comes naturally and overpopulate the palace. However, in the early seventeenth century, when rats and mice began to destroy the silkworm industry in Japan, a royal decree set all cats free to do their thing. Did they save the silkworm industry just as they'd saved the crops in Egypt centuries before? (Does a bear make a noise when it falls down in the woods?) And did the Japanese follow the example of the Egyptians and make them gods? No way! The Emporer was thankful, not crazy. Besides, the Jesuits had just moved into the neighborhood.

Who turned out the lights?

Europe's Dark Ages were darkest of all for our feline friend. He was labeled a "familiar" – an animal form supposedly taken by Satan himself here on earth. The "proof" implicating old *Felis* with Old Scratch, according to the leading intellects of the time, was the dilation and contraction of the pupils of a cat's eyes. Instead of interpreting the changing shapes as a symbol of the waxing and waning of the moon (as the Egyptians did), our European forebears saw them as "the eyes of the devil." Thus were cats found guilty of being couriers from hell. (As my friend Will Cuppy would have said, "This is known as 'The Wisdom of the Ancients.'")

Echoes of this kind of insanity can still be heard in today's world. For example, each year in Belgium, at Ypres, the Cat Festival is held on the second Sunday of May. On that day, hundreds of people dressed as cats (such as Puss in Boots, or the Egyptian cat god, Bast, or Bastet, or Pasht, or Bubastis, or . . . forget it!) march in a festive parade. This event celebrates the following legend: In 962, Baudouin III, count of Flanders, became a convert to Christianity. Because he wanted to demonstrate that he wasn't afraid of the pagan superstition that cats were in league with the Devil, he had two or three of them thrown from the tower of his castle! This ritual was reenacted periodically over the centuries, and then abandoned. But, in

1938, Baudouin's gesture was resumed – but this time using *toy* cats instead of real ones. (Who says we humans aren't making progress?)

The low point in cat history arrived in the late fifteenth century. At that time, cats were even persecuted by the Church! Popes Sixtus IV and Innocent VIII have the dubious distinction of setting public opinion against cats through their edicts condemning witchcraft. Still, since as many people as cats were persecuted during this period, I don't think the medieval establishment meant anything personal by it.

SIDEBAR: Though cats are not mentioned in the Bible, or in the Koran, several quite touching verses regarding Jesus and cats can be found in the Apocryphal Writings of the Gospel of the Holy Twelve – so there.

By the seventeenth century, religious minorities had had enough of prejudice and persecution. Many, like the Pilgrims, sailed into the sunset looking for a new life. Anyway, that's how that famous world traveler, the cat, first arrived in the Americas.

Here's a parallel historical observation. You'll remember that as far back as 3,000 B.C., the ancient Egyptians were very, very nice to cats. Result: the cats controlled the rats and mice, saving the crops in the nation's granaries. Yet, in Europe's dark ages, the Church (and society in general) accused cats of wichcraft, and persecuted them unto death. Result: an explosion of the rat population, and the deadly reign of the Black Plague, which killed a third of Europe's population!

And here's a cat-oriented example of historical *dé já vu*. Here in the U.S.A., almost five thousand years after cats saved Egypt's bacon, hordes of mice and rats were threatening the food supplies and health conditions of remote mining camps in the early days of the California gold rush. The cry for help went out, and in 1849, the sailing ship Ohio arrived in San Francisco with a cargo of several hundred cats, bought on the East Coast for about ten cents apiece. Dockside, in San Francisco, the cats were sold for up to $50 in gold – each! A few weeks later, the plague of rodents was ended, and the Golden State was made safe for traffic jams.

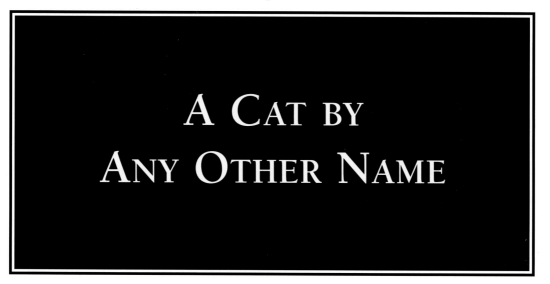

Chapter 4

A Cat by Any Other Name

There are thirty-five species of cats on earth today. (I think maybe God got carried away.) Entire books have been written on the subject of "What breed of cat is right for you?" By all means, read them. You're bound to learn something.

Because cats all tend to look alike, perhaps your first step in choosing a particular cat breed is to go to a cat show, and see for yourself just what your choices are. When you do, you'll discover that cats are all pretty much the same size and shape. In effect, they all fit the universal impression of what a cat is.

(On the other hand, at a dog show you'll see a lot more variety – large and larger; small and smaller; the hairless, the hairy, and the very hairy. Let's face it, there's a lot more contrast at a dog show than at a cat show. Also, dogs seem to really appreciate the fact that you're there to see them. Cats could care less.)

Another basic difference between cats and dogs is the way they view their human owners. According to ethnologists (alleged animal behavior experts) a dog thinks of his owner (whether man or woman) as the leader of the pack – i.e., the dominant male. All right. I can go along with that. But, these same experts claim that cats see *their* owners (again, regardless of gender) as their *mother*!

Hey! Hold the phone! (As my father used to say.) I mean, my cats may not be rocket scientists, but I can't believe they don't know the difference between me and their mother. I think they see me as a convenient, but not necessarily essential, provider. In a phrase: an opener of cans.

However, the overriding truth regarding cat ownership is this: no matter what breed (or non-breed) of cat you might be considering, remember, *they're all cats!* And a cat – with all the behavioral characteristics that that word entails – is what you're going to end up with. Not a dog, not a budgie, but a cat!

For example, cats do most of the things they do because they are innocent creatures of habit; driven by instinct. (Unlike people, who do most of the things *they* do because they're perverse.)

Feline Fitness . . .

When it comes to fitness, cats are always in shape. They need very little help from you. The fact is, cats have a built-in, natural, and quite effective exercise program. It's called stretching. It just so happens, the way the muscles of the cat are structured and interconnected, in one long, leisurely stretch, a cat enjoys the full effect of a total exercise program. Honest!

In fact, you could lock your cat up in your mailbox for a month, feed and water it regularly, and as long as it had room to stretch, it would be in the same tip-top shape when it came out as when it went in. (No, I've never tried it. And no, I don't know what you'd do about getting your mail.)

Even when taking a nap, a cat's body is busy repairing cell tissues. Muscle is actually being rebuilt. It's that kind of conditioning that allows a cat to jump *five times* its own height (assuming it has the proper motivation).

The good old days . . .

At thirteen years old, Sadat is our oldest cat. Nowadays, the average cat lives to be about sixteen. But while a cat is considered to be old at fourteen years, at least one lived to be thirty-six! So, if you sort of like cats, but you really don't want to spend half your life with one, pick out an average cat.

Speaking of old age, two warning signs that a cat is nearing the end of its life are excessive drinking and frequent urination. (Come to think of it, those same symptoms apply to half the guys I hang out with up at Poor Henry's saloon.) And according to one cat-care booklet, "If a cat's fur stands on end all the time, it's probably a sign of stress." Terminal stress, I'd say.

By the way, anyone in the market for a cat should know that blue-eyed, pure white cats are almost always deaf. However, these same cats are also noted for their above average intelligence. (Meanwhile, pink-eyed, pure white specimens with exceptionally long, floppy ears are usually rabbits.) And speaking of strange-looking cats, one in particular will always live in my memory as unique.

One of a kind . . .

Nancy and I were living in the Cobble Hill section of Brooklyn at this time (we're talking B.C. family history here – i.e., Before Children). One afternoon, as we were leaving our house, we saw an animal sauntering down the sidewalk toward us. My first impression was that it was a stray dog. But after doing a double-take, I realized it was a cat! At least, I was pretty sure it was a cat.

To begin with, he was the tallest cat I've ever seen. And lanky too. And while his

21

tail and most of his body seemed to have patches of hair rather than a normal coat, he did have something resembling a lion's mane around his neck and chest. His coloring was so vague and atonal as to be indescribable. He was awkward. He was ridiculous. He was absolutely scruffy.

Scruffy! I knew I'd found just the right name for him the second I thought of it! Crouching down on the sidewalk, I said softly, "Scruffy, Scruffy. Kittykittykitty," using the strained falsetto voice we all affect when attempting to communicate with a cat. At the sound of my voice, Scruffy stopped, and looked up at me. I think I screamed.

In addition to all of his other peculiar qualities, Scruffy was cross-eyed. Not a little cross-eyed mind you, but cross-eyed to a fault! And to top it off, each of his misdirected eyes was a different color! Looking at him straight on; full-face, was akin to a spontaneous psychedelic experience.

Trying to stifle our laughter, Nancy and I petted him and talked to him for a few moments. "Would you like to live with us" we asked. He was friendly enough, even affectionate. However, perhaps remembering a previous appointment, Scruffy soon turned from us to resume his journey.

As he passed Daisy's Market, the big German shepherd always tied to the door jamb went into his cat-intimidation routine: barking, lunging, snarling, straining on the leash to reach this impudent intruder. Scruffy didn't even look at him. Nor did he change his sauntering pace as he walked out of our life forever.

Although disappointed – deep down, Nancy and I understood. Scruffy was not Pygmalion material. He didn't need us, or anyone. His home was his environment, and he was content with his place in it. We wished Scruffy well on his life's journey, but we never forgot him. And to remember him is to smile.

Chapter 5

GAUGING YOUR CAT TEMPERATURE, AND OTHER TOPICS

It suddenly occurs to me that, before you decide what kind or how many cats to invite into your life, perhaps you should ask yourself this question: "Do I have what it takes to be a cat person?" (The incorrigibly sardonic Ambrose Bierce probably didn't. In his Devil's Dictionary, he defines cats as:

> "Cat, *n*. A soft, indestructible automaton provided by nature to be kicked when things go wrong in the domestic circle.")

As it turned out, even my Italian-born grandfather was ambivalent about cats.* In one of the last conversations we had before his death, I asked the eighty-three-year-old former coal miner if he had ever owned any cats.

*On the other side of my heritage, my paternal, Irish-American grandfather, Edward Douglas Denny, felt the same way about people.

Enrico, who, along with his *esposa,* Aufgusta, had successfully raised seven *bambina* and one *bambino* in abject (but apparently not too oppressive) poverty, was one of the wisest and most cheerful individuals I've ever known. Smoking his ever-present pipe, he thought my question over. "No," he said, "no cats." "But *Po-Po*," I protested, "I remember you always had a dog for hunting – why don't you like cats?" "I like cats," he said indignantly. "Well then," I persisted, "how come you never had a cat?" His marvelous brown eyes danced as he answered. "I never had any mice!"

Once is not enough . . .

Statistics tell us there are more cats in the world than dogs. I don't mean to imply anything by that. It's just a fact. Actually, according to the latest U.S. census, there are around *fifty million* cats in this country alone! And over *ten million* American households have *more* than one cat!

That being the case, here's a question every potential (and actual) cat owner will have to confront at some point, "What is the ideal number of cats appropriate to a household?" This very contemporary topic was addressed in the early thirteenth century in the <u>Ancren Riwle</u> (*The Rule of the Anchoresses)*: a medieval treatise written for the guidance of women who were trying to live a strict religious life.

In addition to admonishing women to work hard and "avoid gossiping," the obviously sexist authors counseled them to limit their pets to "but one cat." Far be it from me to argue with the medieval theological mind, but, personally, I have always held if you're going to have *one* cat, there's simply no reason not to have *two.* Not from a food expense standpoint, or a litter box standpoint, or any other standpoint I can think of.

With two, the cats can keep each other company. They can play with each other when no one is home. Anyway, two of *anything* is usually more amusing than just one. In fact, to anyone who has but one cat, and that cat is, for whatever reason, a problem, I have only one piece of advice: get another cat!.

Now, when you analyze the question of "how many cats" further, you'll soon find yourself agreeing with Nancy and me that having *three* cats is really no more trouble or expense than having two, which, as we have already demonstrated, has several advantages over having just one. And, upon further reflection, is there any difference between having three versus having *four*? (I think I'd better end this little exercise here. We've had as many as eight at a time. Admittedly, eight is a little crazy. On the other hand, Mark Twain had eleven cats, and who ever heard of a crazy writer?)

Inside out . . .

Which brings us to the admittedly sensitive question of raising cats as indoor/outdoor or strictly indoor cats – assuming you have the option. Of course, millions of cat owners do not. In which case, there's no decision to make. But, if you *do* have the option . . .

There are arguments to be made on both sides. For example, by allowing your cat to be an indoor/outdoor cat; living a part of its life in a natural environment, you run the risk of your cat being afflicted with fleas, ear mites, fight bites, infections, worms, auto accidents, ticks, and outrageous fortune. On the other hand, by making your cat a strictly indoor cat, you eliminate the possibility of ticks and auto accidents. Probably.

The biggest negative in raising your cat as an indoor/outdoor switch hitter is the ever-present possibility of injury – especially from that fossil-fueled dinosaur of our day, the automobile. Take Tristan's case for example . . .

Wherever he goes, Tristan carries around with him an ounce or two of stainless steel. His pelvis was broken in 1988, when he had an early morning dispute with a car regarding the right-of-way on the county road which passes right in front of GlenDenny. A few weeks (and over $800) later, I made the mistake of observing to the veterinarian, "At least Tristan has learned his lesson. I'll bet it'll be a cold day in Casablanca before he tries to cross that road again." The good doctor gave me a look of bemused incredulity. "Oh no," he said. "Cats never learn anything from these kinds of experiences." Marvelous.

I'm happy to report that today, all these years later, the operation hasn't interfered with Tristan's lifestyle in the least. And either he's stayed on his own side of the road these last few years, or he's been leading a charmed life. And was he worth the $$ investment? I almost always think so.

(None of the other cats play with Tristan. This is because Tristan's idea of playing is a little rough on the playmate in question. He doesn't mean to be mean, it's just that he's The King, and *he* makes the rules.)

The other major source of outdoor cat injuries is *bad cats*. (A bad cat is defined as any cat [other than your own] who makes trouble for you and yours.) When we first moved to GlenDenny, there was a stray unaltered male in the neighborhood who went out of his way (*way* out of his way) to make life miserable for us. All of us. (He was so aggressive, he even attacked poor old Missy, who always stayed by the house!)

Finally, after shelling out over $300 on vet fees for infected bite wounds, scratch wounds, and psychological stress (suffered by Nancy and myself, *as well* as the cats) we'd had enough. So, we called the town animal warden, who stopped by the next day and gave us a (humane) trap to set. Within 24 hours, the unrepentant perpetrator had been caught, and taken away by the authorities to reflect on his sociopathic behavior.

Lastly, here's one more small, but significant, factor to consider when deciding the indoor/outdoor question. Your cat; my cat; *any* cat, would rather do his or her business outdoors than anywhere else. It's so much more *fun* for them. A box of kitty litter, though functional, just doesn't have the sensual mystique and raw adventure offered by the great outdoors. For the average cat, dead leaves and dirt beat out scented cat litter six ways to Sunday.

(It's Pizza who seems to have the biggest problem conducting her toilette in exposed settings. The problem's name is Scamper. Seems like every time Pizza picks out and prepares her chosen little patch of comfort and settles in, eyes half shut, Scamper will suddenly rush out from behind a nearby bush in a ferocious mock attack. This usually results in Pizza running back to the house and making use of the more mundane facilities in the basement.)

Seriously, in making our decision to "Let cats be cats," Nancy and I have weighed in the balance the heartbreak of a precious life ended too soon – versus the multi-dimensional stimulations and rewards offered by a free lifestyle. Because we feel we have a special environment here on our almost-acre with its little woods and wilds, we choose freedom for our children. Freedom to roam, to explore, to hunt. Freedom to hang around the house, like Pizza – or to wander off for two or three days at a time, like Sadat.

Still, I recognize that some of my readers may not agree. So, in defense of the "Let cats be cats" option, I call to the stand Dr. Bruce Fogle, D.V.M., who, in his recent best-selling (serious) cat book, Know Your Cat, points out, "Indoor cats are often prone to spray around inside the home to demonstrate frustration for not being allowed to mark territory outdoors." Also, Dr. Fogle observes that a cat's outdoor territorial wandering "keeps him trim . . . and stimulates his mind." (I'll agree with half that statement.)

Indoor versus outdoor – assuming the right circumstances, it's a decision we all have to make. But as for me, on a quiet afternoon, when I look out the second-story window of my home office and see Tristan lying in the sun, flat on his back, his white tummy exposed for all to see, I am content we've made the right decsion.

(It's been suggested that when a cat lies flat on his back, with its legs spread toward

27

the sky, it is an open invitation for you to play with him. The last time I approached Scamper lying in that posture, he immediately jumped up and ran into the woods. One can only assume it is not a universal invitation.)

Let's wrap up the question of gauging one's natural affinity for cats by approaching it from the more clearly-defined negative side. You can be assured you are definitely *not* a potential cat person if:

1. You demand obeisance from all creatures, human or otherwise, in your presence.
2. Keeping your grandmother's sofa in pristine condition is the greatest goal of your life.
3. You feel it's only reasonable for your cat to not only learn to use the toilet, but flush it as well.
4. You live in a rough part of town and are thinking of getting a cat for protection.
5. You honestly believe that there is nothing in the whole world cuter than a baby chipmunk – and that any beast bloodthirsty enough to bite its little head off is an agent of the Evil One.

And speaking of hunting . . .

Chapter 6

UNDERSTANDING THE PERENNIAL PROWLER

Let me be very clear on this often controversial subject. To a cat, hunting is *not* a form of idle entertainment. It is a basic instinct! And while you can take the cat out of nature, *you can't take the nature out of the cat!*

In support of my thesis, I call upon a former Presidential candidate, the late Adlai E. Stevenson. While Governor of my old home state of Illinois, the eloquent Mr. Stevenson, a certified egghead and unabashed cat lover, vetoed a piece of legislation entitled: "<u>An Act to Provide Protection to Insectivorous Birds by Restraining Cats</u>."

In his veto statement, Adlai said, "I veto and withhold my approval from this bill for the following reasons: It would impose fines on owners and keepers who permitted their cats to run at large off their premises. It would permit any person to capture, or call upon the police to pick up and imprison, cats at large. It would

29

permit the use of traps. The bill would have statewide application – on farms, in villages, and in metropolitan centers.

"This legislation has been introduced in the past several sessions of the legislature, and it has, over the years, been the source of much comment – not all of which has been in a serious vein. It may be that the General Assembly has now seen fit to refer it to one who can view it with a fresh outlook. Whatever the reasons for passage at this session, I cannot believe there is a widespread public demand for this law, or that it could, as a practical matter, be enforced.

"Furthermore, I cannot agree that it should be declared public policy of Illinois that a cat visiting a neighbor's yard or crossing the highway (*hey, Tristan!*) is a public nuisance. It is in the nature of cats to do a certain amount of unescorted roaming (*ah there, Sadat!*). Many live with their owners in apartments or other restricted premises, and I doubt we want to make their every brief foray an opportunity for a small game hunt by zealous citizens – with traps or otherwise. I am afraid this bill could only create discord, recrimination, and enmity.

"Also consider the owner's dilemma: To escort a cat abroad on a leash is against the nature of the cat, and to permit it to venture forth for exercise unattended into a night of new dangers is against the nature of the owner. Moreover, cats perform useful services, particularly in rural areas, in combatting rodents – work they necessarily perform alone and without regard to property lines.

"We are all interested in protecting certain varieties of birds. That cats destroy some birds, I well know, but I believe this legislation would further but little the worthy cause to which its proponents give such unselfish efforts.

"The problem of cat versus bird is as old as time. If we attempt to resolve it by legislation, who knows but we may be called upon to take sides as well in the age-old problems of dog versus cat, bird versus bird, even bird versus worm. In my opinion, the State of Illinois and its local governing bodies already have enough to do without trying to control feline delinquency.

"For these reasons, and not because I love birds the less or cats the more, I veto and withhold my approval from Senate Bill #93."
That's telling 'em Gov!

Now, after reading Mr. Stevenson's reasoned, enlightened, and unassailable objections against restricting the outdoor movements of a cat (dogs, admittedly, pose an entirely different problem), you might assume that the issue of municipal cat control in the U.S. has been resolved, once and for all. HA! Would you believe that here – right here in East Hanover, NJ, the Gateway to Morris County – the Town, in its un-infinite wisdom, has set a parallel and perilous collision course with local defenders of *Felis Domestica*? Behold:

Section 173-24. Running at Large; Trespassing on Private Property.
"A. No person owning, keeping, or harboring any animal shall suffer or permit it to run at large upon the public streets or in any public park or in any public building or in any public place within the Township.
"B. No person shall permit any animal in his care or custody or under his control, whether or not on a leash, tether, cord, chain or the like, to enter upon or defecate upon the lawn, yard or entrance walk or driveway of any private residence without the permission of the owner or tenant thereof."

To add injury to insult, this benighted attitude flows from the same bureaucratic mindset that just two years ago bestowed upon all the cat owners in town the exquisite opportunity to pay a licensing fee of $7.00 for every feline owned, kept, or harbored. Nancy and I were then, and remain today, underwhelmed!

It was ever thus, dear reader. In the arena of life, while there are a paucity of permanent victories, there remain an *abundance* of unjust causes worthy of striving against. As Pogo's friend Howland Owl (or was it Albert the Alligator?) was wont to say: "I'd write a nasty letter to my congressman, if only he could read."

J.R.'s story

If only he could *speak*, Clarissa's iguana, J.R., would bear unimpeachable witness to my earlier observation that, *while you can take the cat out of nature, you can't take the nature out of the cat!*

About eight months ago, someone left open the door to Clarissa's bedroom where J.R. reigns. (At that time J.R. was just an adolescent, about 11 inches long – from the horns on his little green snout, to the tip of his [detachable] mottled tail.)

We suspect that a certain black cat here at GlenDenny – whose identity will remain anonymous – discovered the open door, walked in, and introduced himself to J.R. By the time Nancy stumbled onto the scene a minute or so later, she found traces of blood on the floor, and a few inches of a familiar mottled tail lying under the chair.

(Even though the prime suspect was nowhere in sight, the scene was reminiscent of the famous James Thurber cartoon: An angry woman, arms akimbo, in a peaceful, country setting is confronting an enormous hippopotamus. A man's shoe, a pipe, and a hat are lying at its feet. Caption: *"What Have You Done with Dr. Millmoss?"*)

But fear not, dear reader. You'll be happy to hear that, aside from the lamentable loss of one-third of his tail, and miscellaneous scratches, J.R. did survive. You'll also be relieved to learn that, in the ensuing months, (1) J.R.'s tail has grown back (just the way nature designed), and (2) J.R. himself has almost *doubled* in size. As a result, when that same anonymous black cat once again managed to sneak into Clarissa's room recently, what he saw stopped him short. After sizing up the now formidable J.R., Mr. Anonymous, mustering all the dignity at his command, turned, and exited the room.

In addition to giant iguanas, there's at least one other self-protected species around here which even the most avid hunters among our cats draw the line at tackling: the crows. Blue Jays? Maybe. Crows? No way. (The crows are probably one of the last ecological links to what it might have been like living here two hundred years ago. Their incessant [and insistent] calls are often the first sounds Nancy and I hear in the morning.)

Of course, some of our cats exhibit more intense hunting characteristics than others. Whereas Bart and Tristan are true reflections of the poet's observation, *"Nature, red of tooth and claw,"* Sadat, Scamper, and Punkie just seem to go through the motions, probably to keep their license to hunt valid. Predictably, Pizza is completely above the whole subject. However, on occasion, she will stalk her own tail relentlessly.

The hallmark of any great hunter is patience. My friend Whitey, a former fixture at Poor Henry's Saloon, has a cat named Tammy who definitely falls into the red tooth/red claw category. According to Whitey, he and Tammy were napping on the sofa one day after dinner when he (Tammy) caught a glimpse of a mouse scurrying into the hall closet. Tammy investigated, but came up empty. However, he *knew* Mr. Mouse *had* to be in that closet somewhere. So, Tammy stationed himself on the other side of the half-open door, and waited.

It was a long wait. One day passed. Then another. Still Tammy remained at his post. Finally, after three days, the elusive interloper emerged from the depths of the closet – confident of his safety after his long retreat. (Surprise!) When it was all over, Tammy and Whitey were finally able to get some sleep.

Of course, one way to keep a cat's hunting instinct in control is to keep him or her fat and happy – literally. The fact is, many cat owners upset the balance of nature by feeding their cats too much. And though most cats have enough common sense not to allow themselves to be force-fed, others do eventually learn to become overeaters. And a few *insist* on it.

Living to eat . . .

Some cats enjoy eating so much, they never get enough — at least that's what *they* think. Pizza is a classic example of the compulsive eater. She'd rather eat than . . . well, than anything. At dinner time, we feed her in a separate room, behind closed doors, or else she'd make lightning raids on the plates of the others. (Even Tristan won't get in Pizza's way when she's on a feeding frenzy.) And, just to complicate matters, some cats have certain foods that register right off the Richter scale as far as their taste buds are concerned.

Our Cali (short for Calico) was a small female who had survived distemper as a kitten. Perhaps as a lingering effect of this early illness, Cali developed an *insane* craving for fresh shrimp. Whenever I cleaned shrimp (definitely not one of my favorite cooking chores), *nothing* could stop Cali from leaping onto the kitchen counter top and hurling herself into the shrimp-filled colander.

I tried water pistols. I tried pushing her off the counter. I tried throwing her out of the kitchen — nothing fazed her. In the end, my only defense against her fanatical compulsion was to lock her in the pantry even before I brought the s-h-r-i-m-p into the house!

The late, great Dandy felt almost as intensely about bone marrow — but he usually restrained himself long enough for me to get it onto a plate. Usually.

Among the current generation of cats at GlenDenny, the nearest thing to a food obsession is Bart's love of potato chips — plain, Bar-B-Que, even Sour Cream and Chives. The softest rustle of the bag being opened is enough to bring Bart to the scene of the snack.

34

Chapter 7

INTRODUCING YOURSELF TO YOUR CAT

Your first job as the owner of a cat is to provide an appropriate name for the new member of your family. Of course, if you've gotten an older cat who already has a name, you've saved yourself what can be a frustrating experience – especially when other, less perceptive, members of the family insist on second-guessing your *nom-de-chat*.

(Just be glad that you don't have to name a thoroughbred racing horse. In that situation, the colt's name must reflect the names of *both* parents. For example, if the equine parents in question were named *Southern Dancer* and *Hot Sounds*, you might name the colt *Jazzy Two-Step* – or you might not.)

Anyway, in naming a cat, you can make any rules you want. Or you don't have to make any rules at all. As for me, I have only one rule: the cat's name has to have *something* to do with the cat itself.

35

Pizza is "Pizza" because, as I've explained, she was found abandoned at a nearby pizza franchise. And as for Cleopatra, she got her name because she was so beautiful and exotic, and because we had named her companion "Sadat," in honor of the late Egyptian president. (Come to think of it, when I named Sadat "Sadat," I seem to have broken my own cat-naming rule. Oh well, that's what rules are for.)

Our Tristan (which means "sad warrior") got his name from his poignant expression, and Scamper is "Scamper" because he was so frisky – scampering all over the room when Nancy and I picked him out at the animal shelter in East Hanover. Our orange tabby "Punky" is short for Pumpkin. And Bart, our black cat, is named for Black Bart, the California highwayman active in the last century.

I remember once in the early seventies when the name of our lovely calico, Rosebud, was the subject of some intense consternation. (We called her "Rosebud" because of her pretty pink nose.) A moving company was delivering some of our furniture, and I was directing the mover down to the basement where a particular table was to be placed. As we started down the stairs, I noticed Rosebud, taking a little nap right at our feet. "Come on, let's go, Rosebud," I said, picking her up. "Rosebud!?!" the mover exclaimed in indignation, "That's my *mother's* name!"

Periodically, throughout the afternoon, I could hear the offended party mumbling to himself, "Imagine that. Naming a cat Rosebud! A damn cat!"

Have you met Miss Jones?

Every book on cats has a chapter on "How to introduce a new cat to the household." They recommend that you choose a young animal, that for several days, you keep it separated from the cat(s) already there. They also suggest that you monitor the acceptance, or lack of it, of the newcomer when it's finally allowed to move freely around the house. Now, all that's fine as far as it goes. But . . .

When Missy first entered our lives in 1966, we were living in San Francisco. I'd picked her up off the street one morning on my way to catch the Hyde Street cable car (hence her name, befitting a woman of the streets). Missy was a young, gray tabby who seemed unusually friendly, and was purring loudly* as I carried her back to our apartment.

In order to avoid a premature confrontation between Missy and our long-haired orange tabby (a large altered male named Pekoe – as in Orange Pekoe) Nancy and I put her in a spare room. (Frankly, we had visions of carnal slaughter as Pekoe ripped into this presumptuous newcomer who had the audacity to claim a place in our lives.)

We kept them apart for two days. During this time, I went around the neighborhood posting "Kitten Found" notices. (This is what is known in the cat business as *The Height of Optimism*.) During all that time, Pekoe kept vigil just outside the bedroom door, hissing malevolently whenever any sound was heard from within. Finally, even though we had our doubts, Nancy and I made the introduction. We opened the bedroom door, and – out rushed Missy, practically knocking over Pekoe in the process. Suddenly, she stopped; turned; saw Pekoe, and threw herself on the hallway carpet.

As she lay stretched out on her side, she dug her claws into the carpet, and making the most obscene noises imaginable, pulled herself along the floor; slithering toward Pekoe like some sort of self-abasing acolyte. Missy was obviously in love. (Even more obviously, she was in heat!) It was all too much for Pekoe. He'd been in love before, but nothing like this! He ran down the length of the long narrow hallway, toward the kitchen, his furry tail a-bristle. This sudden flight from her passion convinced Missy to abandon the subtle approach, and switch to the direct approach. She took off after him – a small, gray ball of intense desire pursuing a fast-fading orange blur.

*Purring is, generally, an indication that a cat is relaxed, confident, and content – but don't count on it. Scamper does some of his most painful biting while purring away like a Mercedes S-350.

For the next several minutes, our little apartment was reminiscent of the Indianapolis Speedway time-trials as Pekoe ran in one room and out the other with Missy staying close on his heels, caterwauling (pardon the expression) in unrequited ecstasy. Whenever poor Pekoe would stop and make a stand to save his honor, Missy would hit the deck and start her snake act again – slithering closer and closer to Pekoe until his nerve broke, and he turned and ran for his life. Nancy and I may have laughed harder in our lives, but I doubt it.

A few days later I got a call from Nancy. (I knew there had to be a problem. Nancy *never* called me at the office.) "What?" I asked with some trepidation. "It's Missy and Pekoe," she whispered, "They're doing it!" "They're doing what?" I asked uncomprehendingly. "It! It!" Nancy yelled. (Thinking Pause) "They can't do that," I protested. "At least *he* can't – he's altered!" "Well, he's doing a pretty good job pretending," Nancy insisted. "And if you don't believe me, ask Missy!"

Just to be sure, Nancy called our vet, who said that such activity was not unusual, and we shouldn't be concerned. "The stork won't be visiting your apartment," he reassured her. Anyway, the next weekend, with the vet's help, we made an honest cat out of Missy.

The art of cat-giving

There comes a time in the life of every cat *aficionado* when immediate circumstances preclude an individual from taking to their bosom every cat or kitten who has inadvertently (or vertently) wandered into his or her life. In these cases, my response has always been the same – yes, provide care and shelter, but, *immediately* seek out a deserving (i.e., unsuspecting) soul to foist the homeless one upon. Clarabell's story is a good example of this technique in action . . .

In October of 1972, we were living in the Cobble Hill (Red Hook) section of Brooklyn. I can't remember the details, but one day I found myself in possession of a dirty little calico kitten. I knew we couldn't keep her because our small home already had its fill of cats.

The next morning, my cat-giving plan went into action when the following note appeared on the employee bulletin board of the large New York City ad agency where I was working:

* EXOTIC OFFERING *

From the Wilds of Red Hook:

CLARABELL . . . THE CUDDLY CALICO KITTEN
(Just 7 weeks old)

*She needs LOVE,
*She needs FOOD,
*She needs a BATH,
*She needs **YOU**!

Delivered right to your desk in a plain brown wrapper.

* ONLY $.35 *
(Because *everybody* is worth *something*!)

CONTACT: D. MICHAEL DENNY - 9th Floor, Ext. 8126

As a result of this little marketing ploy, within two hours, I got a call from a young lady in the Traffic department. She had just gotten an apartment, and would *love* to provide a good home for little Clarabell. I explained to her that the kitten really didn't have a name yet, and so she could name her anything she wished. "Oh, I've always loved the name Clarabell," she replied. Obviously, I had found the perfect owner for the little tyke.

Chapter 8

BEHAVIOR IN CATS (ACCEPTABLE AND OTHERWISE)

As we've already discovered, ethnology is the science of how animals learn and react in life. Therefore, an advanced degree in this discipline makes the ethnologist an expert on animals in general – including our friend the cat. At least that's the assumption, but I have my doubts. For example, every booklet written by ethnologists on the subject of undesirable cat behavior (i.e., "poor manners") usually begins by their insisting, "cats absolutely do not misbehave solely to spite their owners." What *I* want to know is, how can these alleged experts be so sure?

I know from experience just how nimble cats can be when they want to be. So, when I see a favorite vase, or my wife's wristwatch, in graceful trajectory toward the unforgiving floor (with a cat watching its fall with fixed fascination), I can't get away from the suspicion that some mishaps involving cats are not accidents at all.

To help you confirm any suspicions you may have regarding approved cat behavior indoors (there are *no* rules for outdoor behavior), here is an official list of cat no-nos in the home – and what our friends, the cat ethnologists say are recommended responses . . .

1. Spraying: Those in the know say a cat sprays urine in order to mark his territory. We are also informed that this act is instinctive, and therefore should not be taken personally – no matter how many times you have to wash off the chaise lounge.

Solution: Protect any likely spray sites by covering the surface with aluminum foil – even if your living room does end up looking like an aluminum mine.

2. Clawing: Here again, this is alleged to be a purely instinctive action. We're told cats do not scratch up your favorite easy chair to sharpen their claws. A cat's claws are *always* sharp. What they're really doing is cleaning them, while leaving their scent on the object at hand at the same time. Now, doesn't that make you feel better about the whole subject?

Solution: Install a scratching post near the scene of the crime. As the cat transfers his scratching habit to the post, move it (the post) further and further away from the valued object. This would appear to be a logical, proven-effective solution – on paper. Here's another. If you *know* you're going to be really upset by a few rips and tears in the family furniture – yet you insist on having a cat – buy a hamster instead, and use your imagination.

3. Jumping onto high places: Well, here we go again. You just can't fight those natural instincts. Being on top of something – on top of anything – is very big with cats. There are two reasons for this: (1) it makes them feel secure (i.e., in that they have an edge on the world) and (2) they like the view.

(Unfortunately, in the outdoor environment, some cats carry their attraction to heights to extremes. This compulsion results in the frenzied gathering of ladders, and risking of life and limb by the duly appointed rescuer [guess who]. The consequences of these high-wire shenanigans are nearly always the same: one slightly shaken cat and one grumpy rescuer – the reluctant recipient of several painful, panic-induced scratches.)

Solution: Every time your cat jumps on anything higher than a doorstop, say, "No! No! No!" in a firm, but controlled, voice, and set it back down on the floor. Repeat as necessary, but try and get at least four hours of sleep every night.

4. Aggression (i.e., biting, scratching, ambushing): While these actions may or may not be instinctive, they can certainly be painful to the object of the aggression.

Solution: (Preferred.) Check with your local shelter and get the opinion of the pros. I know someone who had a very aggressive cat – to the point that her arms looked like she had been rolling around in bramble bushes. An animal behaviorist suggested she blow gently on the cat. (No, she didn't say where.) Guess what? It worked! From a terrorizing hellion, it became a real sweetheart!

(Alternate solution.) Call in the heavy ordinance. Load up the $1.25 ASPCA-approved* water pistol you purchased just for this contingency, and squirt the little perpetrator right in the puss! (Pardon this expression too.) NOTE: To preserve your credibility as the "Injured Party," try not to giggle while doing this.

5. Fighting: Any cat will defend itself. Even a two-week-old kitten will try and defend itself when it feels threatened. (In contrast, a puppy will assume a submissive posture, while a human baby will look around for help.) Indoors, the conflicts among one's cats tend to be nothing more than spats – little hit-and-run attacks prompted by impulse. In the outdoor arena, however, cats are more aggressive. And some take their aggressiveness on tour around the neighborhood.

*This is what is known as hyperbole.

Solution: If you've got a local bully (probably not neutered) beating up on your little darling, trade in your water pistol for a garden hose. Or, in a worst-case scenario, you may have to arrange for your local animal warden to enroll the miscreant in an attitude adjustment course.

Despite the occasional outburst of admittedly anti-social behavior, recent scientific studies have concluded that – psychologically speaking – cats are well-adjusted animals. At least from their point of view . . .

SIDEBAR: While it's true that cats are not herd animals (lions excepted), they are always very curious to know where another cat is going, or what it might be up to. As a result, around GlenDenny, it's not unusual to see several of the boys and girls hanging around together. Explanation: nobody wants to miss anything.

Playtime!

There are three categories (pardon **this** expression, too) of cat play:

1. Play fighting
2. Object play
    and
3. Just-for-the-hell-of-it play (known in the trade as "Horseplay")

Play fighting always involves two cats, and is defined by the period of time it takes for the *Play* Fighting to turn into *Plain* Fighting! (Usually about 1.3 seconds.)

In Object play, a small ball, or a Widdily (see next page), or a wedding ring, or some other inexpensive and totally replaceable object is batted about until it winds up under a radiator, or gets stuck behind the sideboard, or falls through a crack in the floor, to be lost forever.

Finally, there's the *Just-for-the-hell-of-it* variety of cat play. Picture a cat walking nonchalantly across the lawn, then suddenly leaping straight into the air, doing a 180-degree turn, landing, and running up a tree as though being chased by his worst nightmare. This last form of play might lead an observer to conclude that, in addition to its other qualities, a cat has a vivid imagination. On the other hand, it might not.

(I've read that most of the moves and strategies found in the martial arts were inspired by the graceful agility of the cat. Those Chinese don't miss a thing.)

One of the most time-tested and inexpensive props you can provide to encourage object play is the old-fashioned paper bag.* You know, the kind you bring the groceries home in. Nothing excites a cat's imagination or expectations more than a dark nook or cranny. But, when it comes to making your cat *really* happy, here's

The *Perfect* Cat Toy

Introducing **The Widdily** . . .

Combines all the best qualities of a ball of yarn and a dead mouse! Here's how you can make Widdilies for your cat right in the privacy of your own home!

1. Buy a package of pipe cleaners (the soft, fuzzy kind, not the abrasive variety.)

2. Sit next to your cat and take one pipe cleaner out of the package and hold it up. (This gets Foo-Foo's attention.)

3. Bend the ends in, and wrap it two or three times around your index finger.
   Congratulations! You have now made a Widdily!

*Remember, I said a **paper bag**.

4. Get you cat's attention again, and throw the Widdily across the floor. If your cat doesn't chase it and bat it around the room, make an appointment for him at the vet.

Another inexpensive and all-natural "toy" your cat is sure to enjoy is the ubiquitous walnut – in the shell. It's light enough for even a kitten to bat around, and it clatters as it rolls across wooden floors, which just adds to the excitement. Also, dust balls and dirt wash right off.

Let's play Doctor . . .

One thing you'll have to learn as a cat owner is how to make your cat swallow a pill. You probably already know the existing, universally approved method:

1. Point his nose upward toward the ceiling
2. Drop the pill over the back of the tongue
3. Close his mouth

Regarding the mechanics of medication, whoever thought up that method never put themselves in the cat's place. To prove my point, place a pill in your hand, now, point your nose upward toward the ceiling, drop the pill over the back of your tongue, and close your mouth. We'll continue as soon as you stop gagging. [pause] OK?

Well, after that little experiment, I think you'll agree, there's got to be a better way! We've got to use our imagination here! We have to take advantage of some of the routine behavioral characteristics of *Felidae* and put them to work for us in getting that little pill down the hatch.

For example, since all cats sleep a lot,* all cats yawn a lot. And with a little practice, a little patience, a simple soda straw, (and a lot of pills), I'll bet you could become very adept at zipping that little pill right between the incisors. Oh, you don't have to worry about hitting him in the eye. Cats always close their eyes when they yawn. (Come to think of it, so do I.)

NOTE: In treating a sick cat, remember, while aspirin is great for human ailments, it is absolutely lethal to cats. So if you have a headache, by all means, take a couple of aspirin. On the other hand, if it's a cat that's giving you the headache . . . (I know, I know – that's not very nice.)

Finally, keep in mind that cats do not think of growing older in terms of their "Golden Years." They think of existence in terms of the moment. To them, the past is immutable, and the future inconceivable. Only the *now* is worthy of attention. (In saying that, I may have isolated the quintessential bond that has tied me to cats for all these years. We share the same philosophy: pragmatic fatalism – with a mischievous touch of hedonism.)

A last word on behavior in cats. The unenlightened claim cats are very selfish; demonstrate little desire to please those around them, and are never known to share.** I say so what? People say the same thing about me! What's it prove? Nobody's perfect . . .

---

*According to the experts, the domestic house cat sleeps 16 hours a day on the average. In our household, the only creature that sleeps longer than that is Clarissa.

They **do share, of course. What cat owner has not been thrilled by the sight of a small animal body-part lying at their doorstep, or in the middle of the kitchen floor?

Chapter 9

The Mechanics of the Ordinary House Cat . . .

Featuring *Novus*, the Contemporary Cat©

1. The Nose. A cat's sense of smell is even more extraordinary than its sense of hearing. (Its only greater sense is its sense of dignity.)

2. The Face. Glands on a cat's forehead, chin, and cheeks produce chemicals (pheromones) which allow it to "mark" you with its scent by rubbing against you. (Reminding you of *who* owns *whom*.)

3. The Eyes. Six times more sensitive than the human eye to the blue end of the color spectrum. (However, experts report there is almost nothing worth looking at in that end of the spectrum.)

4. The Brain. According to some, this is where a cat does its thinking. (Or what passes for thinking.)

5. The Ear. American folklore says, "When a cat washes past the tip of his ear with his paw, it means rain is on the way." (Absolutely true – if you're willing to wait long enough.)

6. Eye/Ear. The cat is the only species of animal whose eye movement is conducted independently of its ear movement. (If I knew why, I'd be the first to tell you. I would!)

7. The Unreachable Spot. A spot on the back of the head, which eludes the normal licking process. (While humans don't have any parts that are unreachable, we *do* have some that are unmentionable.)

8. The Whiskers. What appear to be "whiskers" are actually sensing organs, called vibrissae. (Could come in handy if you're ever a contestant on Jeopardy – i.e., "What are vibrissae?")

9. The Teeth. Cats have fewer teeth (thirty at most) than other carnivores. (According to the surviving chipmunks here at GlenDenny, that's plenty!)

10. The Tongue. A cat's tongue is rough and abrasive so it can rasp every teeny bit of meat from the tiny bones of its hapless prey. (Now, aren't you glad I shared that with you?)

11. The Purr-Box. While we know *why* cats purr, we haven't the foggiest notion as to *how* they do it.

50

The Contemporary Cat ...

12. The Claws. All normal (five-toed) cats have eighteen claws: five up front and four in back. It only *feels* like they have more. (Claws also play a key role in the act of "pumping" – a feline form of love/torture inflicted on cat owners.)

13. The Toes. It is not unusual for a cat to have extra toes – that is, more than five. (Such cats disdainfully ignore any jokes on the matter.)

14. The Paws. American folklore: "To keep a cat at home, butter its paws." (This technique actually worked in the 1840s, but not before or since.)

15. The Legs. When walking, a cat's front and hind legs move together – first on one side, then the other! The only other animals that ambulate bilaterally are the giraffe and the camel. (*You* figure it out . . .)

16. The Skeleton. Cats have 244 bones. (If you didn't know that, don't feel bad – neither does a cat.)

17. The Coat. The coat can be striped, blotched, patched, mottled, or solid-colored. Wash in warm water. Do *not* spin dry.

18. The Flea. Of the over 1,600 species of fleas which inhabit our planet, only two are interested in cats. (Unfortunately, they are *very* interested.)

19. The Tail. Provides balance as your cat jumps from the top of the refrigerator to the kitchen counter where you've just left a plate of raw hamburger while you answer the phone. Also useful for communicating cat body language. (And as an endless source of self-amusement.)

20. *Nepeta Cataria (Catnip).* A member of the mint family, whose aroma can have a startling effect on cats. (Almost as startling as the effect of two or three Manhattans on my father-in-law).

21. The Widdily. An easy-to-make cat toy which combines all the best qualities of a ball of yarn and a dead mouse.

22. *Le Divertissement.* Part playmate, part appetizer.

23. The Ball of Yarn. The favorite pastime of cats immemorial.

24. The Goldfish Bowl. The feline equivalent of interactive TV. In this case, *anytime* is prime time!

YOU AIN'T SEEN THE LAST OF *NOVUS* ...

Chapter 10

TRAINING THE COMMON CAT

I read somewhere that, "A cat can be trained to do anything that makes sense to him." All I know is that it took Punky about eight months to learn how to climb down a tree correctly (i.e., backwards). Pizza never has figured it out. (I guess I have to blame myself for being an inept teacher.)

Meanwhile, Tristan, after a night on the town, has his own rather acrobatic way of entering the house in the wee small hours of the morning. I call it his patented, *up-the-June-magnolia-tree-over-the-roofpeak-and-leap-across-to-the-bay-window* routine.

Sound asleep, Nancy and I first learn of it when we are rudely awakened by a dull "thump," followed by a series of plaintive mews. As I pull the covers over my head,

Nancy shuffles slowly over to the bedroom window that looks onto the bay roof where, inevitably, Tristan waits expectantly. (Nancy is much more accommodating to our cats than I am – especially between the hours of midnight and 8 A.M. You might say it's a calling with her. A *calling*, get it?)

As she opens the window, Tristan, purring with self-satisfaction, comes in and leaps onto the bed. Suddenly, I'm startled by the sensation of being nuzzled by a dew-covered cat! When I reach out to push him away, I'm rewarded by having a wet *hand* to match my wet face! "Gethimouttahere!" I yell.

At this point, Tristan usually smooches and loves his mistress, hoping to convince her to provide an early breakfast. (Now while Nancy will be the first to admit that having a cat knead your head with his paws 'n claws is a less than ideal way to start the day – she'd point out that it beats being awakened by a dog licking your face. [Old Sam, the family boxer we once had back in Illinois, just loved Nancy.])

We've all heard of cats being purposefully trained in the use of human toilets. Some even seem to achieve this feat naturally, without any coaxing or training. And while I find this remarkable, nonetheless, I am reminded of what Dr. Samuel Johnson (a historically-certified cat lover) is reported to have said upon seeing a performing dog walk upright on its hind legs. "I am not surprised that he does it well," observed the good doctor, "as much as that he does it at all."

In the Denny household, we have never had a toilet-trained, or toilet-instinctive, cat. However, we have, on occasion, caught Pizza lurking in the shower under suspicious circumstances.

The role of intelligence in training . . .

The role intelligence plays in the training of a cat is a subject of great controversy. Personally, I don't believe *anyone* with an I.Q. over room temperature is going to have much luck at all. Why? Because people of even the most modest intelligence insist on thinking of a cat's mental capacities in *human* terms. In fact, cats do not have intelligence as we know it. What they have is an *eccentric intellect* – as well as a variety of interests. (Most of these interests are general in nature, but some are *very* particular, if not peculiar.)

(Debate on the question of human intelligence has recently been clouded by a controversy concerning the validity of the Bell Curve. In the case of cats, however, the battle lines are drawn between those who hold to an IQ theory based on a Skewed Parabola, and their opponents who espouse the model of an Eternal Oxymoron.)

Intelligence (or the lack of it) aside, if there's a secret to training a cat, it has to be consistent communication. According to a University of Pennsylvania study, "99% of U.S. cat owners speak to their pets every day." (I assume the other 1% are involved in long-running private disputes which will probably require professional counseling before they're resolved.)

However, comlicating the cat-intelligence hypothesis, a California doctor (Dr. D) reports that while dogs can learn two thousand words, cats can learn only twenty-five to fifty words. But, as Dr. B of Texas explains, "That's because we don't spend as much time teaching cats as we do dogs." Somehow I'm not surprised.

But the last word on the subject comes from another noted cat training authority: ". . . if a cat has never learned anything," he reports, "teaching it will be more difficult." Think about it.

Answering the ultimate question . . .

All right. It's time for me to make good on the promise I made to you in the title of this book. I will now reveal to you the secret of "How to get a cat to sit in your lap." I wouldn't be surprised if wars haven't been fought over less . . .

Now, you'll recall, I did give you my assurance that in achieving this remarkable feat I would eschew the use of rude force or drugs. Therefore, no types of restraints (harnesses, belts, etc.), will be employed. Nor shall I suggest you sit under a sprig of catnip. Neither will I suggest you stoop to using an irresistible temptation — such as sewing an anchovy to the end of your nose. No, dear reader! In our quest for success, it will be a fiendishly clever stratagem conceived by the *superior brain* of the human species which will provide the victory over the fickle feline!

How to Get a Cat to Sit in Your Lap

1. Wait until your local weather maven predicts one of the chillier nights of the year. (While Florida residents may have to wait several weeks for just the right conditions, Montanans [Montaners?] [Montanians?] [Montanamanians?], who live in a state with just two seasons [winter and the Fourth of July], can pick practically any night they want.)

2. Around dusk on L-Day, turn off the heat in one room (your choice), and close the door, sealing off the room from the rest of the house. After dinner, bundle up as if you were going out for a pint of chocolate chip ice cream (including gloves and earmuffs). Next, select a subject cat and carry it into the unheated room. (For those of you presently in cat-less circumstances, you're welcome to imagine using our Sadat [you know, the paranoid one] for this experiment. Lots of luck.)

3. Put the cat on the floor, and sit down in the easy chair you had the good sense to place in the room previously. Keep the lights low.

4. Relax. But do not hum, whistle, or giggle.

What will happen next is, the cat will walk over to the door waiting for you to let him out.

(SIDEBAR: All of our cats feature different "Let me out, dummy!" behavior at the door.

56

Sadat, for example, will cry loudly and, looking behind to make sure you are following, lead you from room to room to the one door he wants you to open.

Sheba would go to the door, look up at you, and let out a wail. And when you'd say "No, no," she'd wail louder – still staring at you intently. The wails would continue to get louder and louder every time you said "No." This could be very cute, for a while.

On the basis of *his* technique, Bart may be the most intelligent of our clauter of cats. He opens the door himself. (Well, some doors anyway.) As befits a 211-year-old home, many of our doors feature the original colonial latchs. By standing on his hind legs, Bart can easily reach the latch and trip it open.

[This ability has prompted at least one semi-hysterical episode here at GlenDenny. After having a few drinks in the living room, an elderly dinner guest asked to use our bathroom. Her presumed privacy was suddenly violated when she heard the latch mechanism operate; saw the door swing slowly open, and beheld a large black cat with big yellow eyes curiously observing the scene before him. It took the infusion of another vodka martini before my guest was able to calm down.]

Now Scamper, when he wants to get out, has the maddening habit of [literally] getting under your feet to get your attention. On a least two occasions, I have been a hair's breath away from hurtling down the stairs due to his attention-getting trip-ping tactic. True to form, if you ignore him, he'll bite you on the ankle.

Pizza sits facing the door, turns her head 180 degrees, and stares at you as she whines to be let out [shades of The Exorcist]. That can be a little unnerving, but it's nothing compared to Tristan's tactic.

Tristan will walk to the door, sit down, and, not making a sound, will stare straight ahead at the door for minutes on end – until you are driven to distraction, and compelled to open it. Personally, I'm convinced he's developing his telepathic skills. But I digress. Back to getting a cat to sit in your lap . . .)

When your cat stands at the door and cries to get out (now you know why I suggested you wear earmuffs), you must remain strong and resolute. In a few minutes, he'll figure out that, for some inexplicable reason, he's stuck in this room with you for the foreseeable future. So, he'll look around for a place to settle down comfortably.

The first place chosen will probably be a radiator cover, or some other expected source of heat. Eventually, he'll realize he's not getting any warmer, but, in fact, is getting colder! He will not waste time trying to figure this out. Always the pragmatist, ultimately your cat will decide to sacrifice his dignity to the cause of personal comfort.

Before you know it, he'll walk right over to your chair; scratch at the armrest for a few seconds, and jump into your lap like he's been doing it all his life. Then, after circling around a few times, he'll settle down, and begin grooming himself. At some point he may go so far as to start purring!

Congratulations! You now have a cat sitting in your lap!

Chapter 11

ONE MORE CAT TALE

The Stork that Came to Nest . . .

When it comes to cats, the Denny household has had just one experience with the miracle of birth. When she came into our lives, Rosebud was a very young calico female with the gentlest disposition and the most intriguing, beguiling face of any cat we've ever had. (She had the perennial expression of one who has just seen something outrageous.)

As with Missy, I first met Rosebud on my way to work. Since she was obviously abandoned (you'll never guess why), and I was only a half block away from home, I deposited her with a surprised Nancy, and continued my commute. (We had only two other cats at that time, and Rosebud fit in right away.) The announcement of her pregnancy was made by the vet when we took her in for a checkup. No problem. In fact, we were delighted.

59

Over the next several weeks, we read up on all the literature, and even prepared a birthing place in a spare bedroom closet. It wasn't anything fancy – a simple box with old towels in it. But it was a dark, quiet place; just what the doctor ordered.

One memorable Sunday afternoon, I was lying on the sofa in the living room, watching TV. Suddenly Rosebud, heavy with impending progeny, jumped up on my stomach and began licking her posterior. I took no notice and continued to watch the TV until I heard Nancy saying (in a voice of controlled hysteria): "I think she's having her babies now! On *you!*"

Sure enough, Rosebud, in her instinctive wisdom, had chosen me to be the site of her blessed event! I was flattered, but after giving it a quick thought (a *very* quick thought), I decided to pass on this singular distinction. I carefully got up; carried her to the birthing box – which she accepted reluctantly. Once there she settled in, and without benefit of even one Lamaze class, calmly proceeded to give birth to three kittens: two males (Dandy Lion and Tiger Stripe), and one female (Sweetpea).

The only minor complication came after the birth of the first kitten (Dandy). Rosebud was so proud of what she'd accomplished that she rolled over on her back, and squirmed and purred loudly to show us her sublime satisfaction. That was fine, except we were afraid she'd roll right over on the little fellow and injure him, so we gently brought her attention back to her struggling newborn. She understood immediately, and began licking him clean before presenting us with her other two surprise packages.

She proved to be a great mother to her kindle (litter), and a great cat over the years, especially with our rough-playing toddlers. Incidentally, while we kept Dandy, we shipped his brother and sister – via Allegheny Airlines – to our friends Phil and Carol, both of whom were professors at Penn State University at the time. (Hey, what are friends for? I'd do the same for you . . .)

Celebrate your cat

January 22nd – Answer your Cat's Question Day. Several years ago, Tom Roy and his wife, Ruth, got the feeling that, every once in a while, their cats were looking at them as though they (the cats) had a question to ask. Being an experienced and inveterate originator of holidays, Tom immediately invented Answer Your Cat's Question Day.

Now, if your cat never seems to have a question on the tip of its tongue, perhaps you can suggest a few. But, if your cats, like mine, give you the impression that they already *know* all the answers, you have my permission to ignore the whole thing. Or, the Roys have told me you can call them yourself at (717) 274-8451.

The Month of June – Adopt-A-Shelter-Cat Month. The American Society for the Prevention of Cruelty to Animals (ASPCA) is the originator and sponsor of this very worthy cause. For reasons both obvious and personal, I plan to donate a percentage of the excessive profits generated by this book to the ASPCA. (I've always been a compulsive optimist. I can't help it.)

Finito . . .

In closing, I wish to make clear that this modest treatise was *not* written to produce a universal love of cats among humankind. In the first place, cats don't need it, and in the second place, I realize that my words lack the power to eliminate the inbred enmity of those who dislike cats. Especially those stricken with *ailurophobia*: the persistent, irrational dislike, aversion, or fear of cats (a phenomenon which I believe is held in common by individuals who, in a previous life, were birds, field mice, or chipmunks).*

A reincarnation researcher claims that our pets are often reincarnated relatives from the past – the reborn souls of those who have led "less than perfect" lives. If that's true, it would go a long way toward explaining some of the more bizarre episodes of my life with cats.

Nor do I believe my little exercise will modify the zealotry of those extremists who hold cats as sacred entities. Those fanatical devotees of the genus *Felis catus* who all but worship the ground little padded paws tread upon.

No. This was written for the edification and entertainment of people like you and me (most especially me). Normal, kind-hearted souls who, while admiring cats overall (and certainly not harboring any arbitrary dislike toward felines in general), nonetheless remain troubled by certain persistent inherent characteristics of aloofness and arrogance. (Characteristics, I might add, which mysteriously disappear as the dinner hour approaches.)

My purpose was not to seek a comprehensive understanding of the beast. That would have been a presumption! Instead, I sought to explore how the *owner* of a cat, in the cunning of his or her mind, might contrive to shape a relationship which provides approximately the same degree of satisfaction to the person operating the can opener, as to the consumer of the contents of the can! Is that asking so much?

In closing, I offer a poem I wrote
a few years ago for a
promotional poster.

Amid the thick, dark greenness,
Silent shafts of sunlight conceal,
The Magnificent Peril.
Unseen, yet all-seeing,
It wears its world like a cloak;
Unblinking amber eyes
Fixed on the moment.

The End